Native American
MANDALAS

KLAUS HOLITZKA

Sterling Publishing Co., Inc.
New York

Library of Congress Cataloging-in-Publication Data Available

10 9 8 7 6 5 4 3

Published by Sterling Publishing Company, Inc.
387 Park Avenue South, New York, N.Y. 10016
First published and © in 1998 by Schirner Verlag Darmstadt.
Under the title *Indianische Mandalas*
English translation © 2000 by Sterling Publishing
Distributed in Canada by Sterling Publishing
c/o Canadian Manda Group, One Atlantic Avenue, Suite 105
Toronto, Ontario, Canada M6K 3E7
Distributed in Great Britain by Chrysalis Books
64 Brewery Road, London N7 9NT, England
Distributed in Australia by Capricorn Link (Australia) Pty Ltd.
P.O. Box 704, Windsor, NSW 2756 Australia
Printed in Mexico

Sterling ISBN 0-8069-2881-6

ABOUT THIS BOOK

The beliefs of the Native American Native American respect and regard for Mother Earth and the Great Spirit are reflected in mandalas. For Native Americans, sky and earth, man and nature, the big and the small are inseparably interwoven and all of creation is holy. The 30 mandalas of this coloring book are based on traditional motifs of various Native American tribes. Every coloring pattern is accompanied by an Native American quote, prayer or song, so that picture and word facilitate a deeper insight into the world view of the Native American.

THE ILLUSTRATOR

Klaus Holitzka was born, in 1947, in Neuburg on the Danube. After training in an advertising agency in Frankfurt, he has been working as an independent artist, since 1969. His work is distinguished by a wide variety of applied techniques, visual language and styles. In 1978, he founded his own art publishing house, and since then, he has been working on design of book covers, maps, and art prints. In his spare time, he has been working on classical painting.

MANDALA:

Sand mandala for a heal-
ing ritual of the Navaho
Native Americans

Wisdom does not belong to a single human being. We have to act wisely, but wisdom does not belong to anybody. It is the revelation of old proven ideas and we obtain it when generation after generation explores the laws of nature.

HUNBATZ MEN, MAYA

MANDALA:
Shield of the Plains Native Americans

There is more than one
path
leading to life after life,
there is more than one
path
to love,
there is more than one
path
to find the other half
of the self in an other
human being,
there is more than one
way
to fight the enemy.

A FEMALE NOOTKA NATIVE
AMERICAN

MANDALA:

Sand mandala for a heal-
ing ritual of the Navaho
Native Americans

So manifold are the
wonders
of creation
that this beauty will
never end.
Creation is present (here)
it is present (here), right
now, in you
has always been there.
The world is a miracle.
The world is magic.
The world is love
And it is here, right
now.

CHEYENNE NATIVE
AMERICANS

MANDALA:

Symbol of the
universe

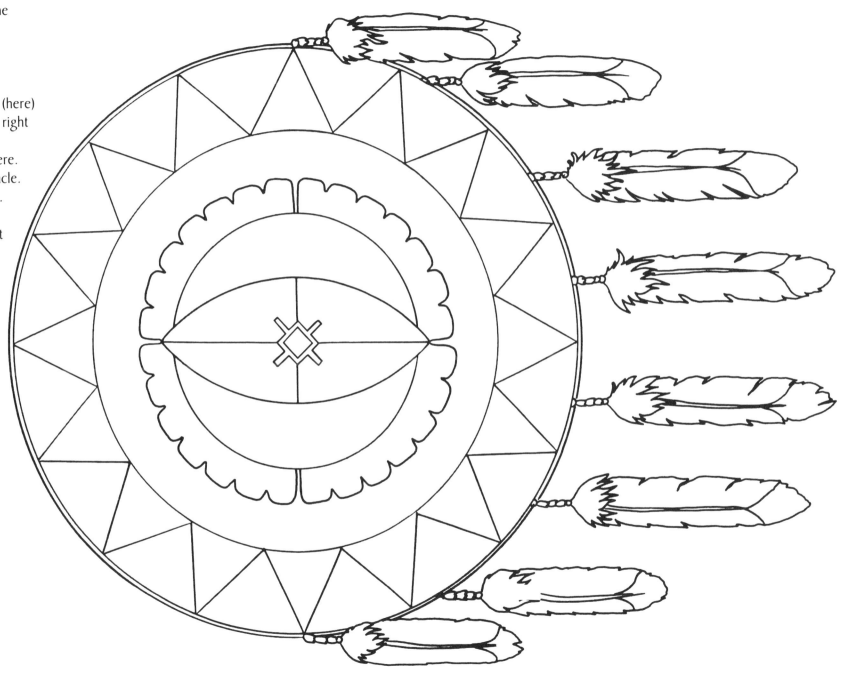

All, all and everything is
of importance
And nothing that is good
happens fast.

SIKWALXLELIX
FEMALE SHAMAN OF THE BELLA
COOLA

MANDALA:

Symbol of the rain deity
Rock drawing of the Hopi
near Betatakin

I don't know whether
the human voice can
reach
to the heavens.
I don't know whether
the Almighty will listen
when I pray.
I don't know whether the
gifts I long for
will be granted to me.
I don't know
whether we can truly hear
the talk
of the ancient.
I do not know all
that might come to pass
in the future.
I hope, my children,
that only good things
will come to you.

Song of the women of the
Pawnee

Mandala:

Collage from symbols of
the Plains Native
Americans.

The books of the white
man are not sufficient for
me.
The Great Spirit has given
me the opportunity
to study at the university
of nature,
the forests and rivers, the
mountains
and the animal world.

Tatanga Mani, Stoney

Mandala:

Representation of duck
wings, Maida Native
Americans, California

Our religion . . . is
written in the hearts
of our people.

<small>CHIEF SEATTLE</small>

MANDALA:

Collage of power animals,
peace pipes and the sun
symbol.

My grandfather gave
simple advice. He recom-
mended to everybody to
ask himself four important
questions that should be
his guidelines.
Am I happy with what
I am doing?
Does what I do
contribute to
the confusion in the
world?
What am I doing for
peace?
How will people
remember me
after I am dead ?

YEHWNODE (TWYLAH
NITSCH)
SENECA

MANDALA:

The four directions
Cheyenne

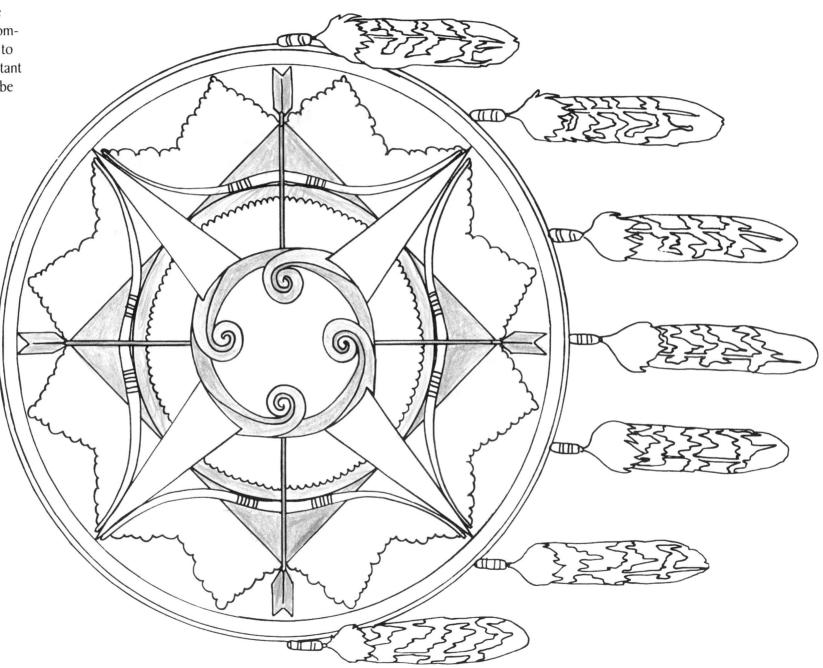

There are no bad days
in the life of an Native
American.
However difficult times
may be - every
day is good.
Because you are alive
every day is good.

HENRY OLD COYOTE
CROW NATIVE AMERICAN

MANDALA:

Thunder arrows of the Navajo

A ll of creation
is holy. Every morning
is holy, every day is
holy because the light of
the day was sent by
Wankan Tanka, our father.
Remember that all crea-
tures
of this world are holy
and therefore
want to be treated
accordingly.

HEHAKA SAPA, SOUIX

MANDALA:

The skunk as symbol of
the sun, Hopi (Native
Americans)

Holy Mother Earth, the trees
and all of nature bear witness
to your thoughts and workings.

WINNEBAGO

MANDALA:
The Great Mother,
Navaho

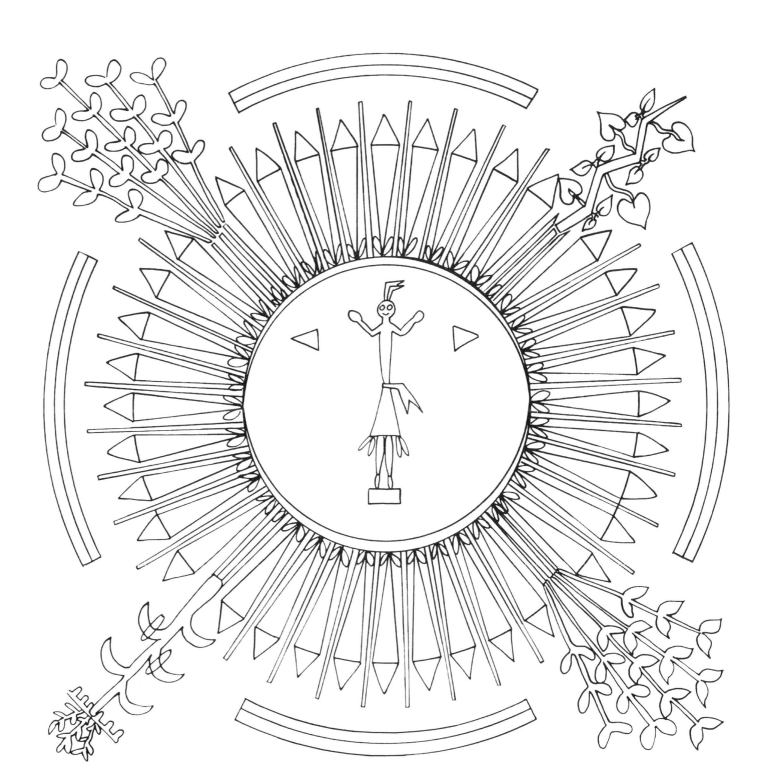

Look at me - I am poor and naked, but I am the chief of
my people. We do not want riches but we want
to bring up our children right. Riches would not be
of any use to us. We cannot take them into the
other world. We do not want riches. We want
peace and love.

RED CLOUD, SIOUX

MANDALA:

After a motif by Mariano Valadez, a Huichol Native American from Mexico.

The earth is beautiful,
the sky is beautiful,
my people are beautiful,
my heart is full of joy.
Whatever is worth
living for
that is also worth
dying for.
Hokahey!

JOHN LAUGHING WOLF

MANDALA:

Sun dance symbol with
forked trees, Plains
Native Americans

We are all flowers
in the garden of the Great
Spirit.
We have a common root:
Mother Earth.
The garden is beautiful
because it
has many flowers: The
colors
of the many traditions and
cultures.

DAVID MONONGYE, HOPI

MANDALA:

Forked blossoms of duali-
ty, Cheyenne

Stillness is calmness
or physical, psychological
and spiritual
harmony.
A person who remains
true
to himself (or herself)
walks
quietly and unperturbed
through all
storms of life.
If you ask :"What is
stillness?" he (or she) will
answer:
"It is the great mystery.
The holy stillness is
His voice."
 And if you ask:
"What are the fruit of stillness?"
he (or she) will answer:
Self discipline, true
courage,
endurance, patience, dig-
nity and respect. Stillness
is the cornerstone of
character."

OHIYESSA (DR. CHARLES
EASTMAN)
SANTEE-SIOUX

MANDALA:

Representation of a tor-
nado, whose eye is
untouched and calm,
Apache Native
Americans.

Together
with all creatures
we were put on this earth,
even the smallest of
grasses
and the largest trees
are part of our family.
We all are brothers and
sisters
and have the same worth
on this earth.

THANKSGIVING PRAYER OF THE
IROQUOIS

MANDALA:

Sand mandala of the
Navahos for the protec-
tion of the herds.

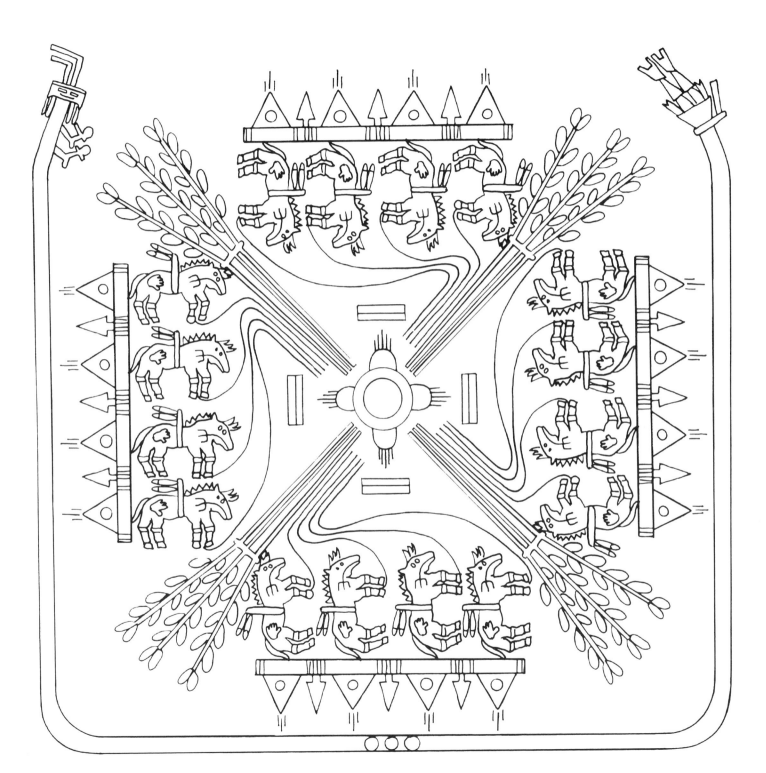

If you rise
in the morning
give thanks for the light of
the morning,
for life and your
strength.
Give thanks for your food
and your joy
in life.
If you do not see any rea-
son
to give thanks
then it is your fault.

TECUMSEH, SHAWNWEE

MANDALA:

Woven plate of the
Navahos for the ritual
preservation of holy food.

In the house of long life,
there I live.
In the house of happiness,
there I live.
Beauty below me,
there I live.
Beauty above me,
there I live.
Traveling to old age
with him I live.
I am on the good path
there I live.

SONG OF THE NAVAHO

MANDALA:

The house of the bear
and the snake, healing
picture of the Navaho.

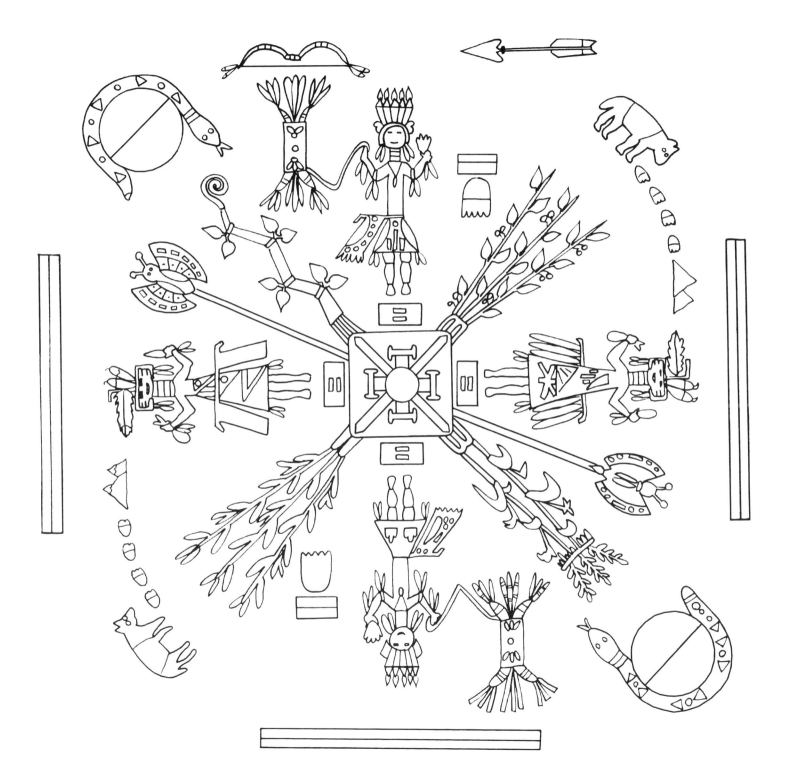

The Great Spirit lives in all,
he animates all (forms) and gives energy to all creations,
including life on earth. This thought is the essence of what White Buffalo Woman taught us and the essence of Native American spirituality. The ancient teachings demand from us that we focus our attention most of all on the holy web of life we are part of and that obviously enmeshes us. This attention to the whole is what my people call holiness.

BROOKE MEDICINE
EAGLE, CROW

MANDALA:

Symbol of the Cheyenne for the interconnected-ness of the four corners.

The people living on this planet have to give up their narrow concept of "freedom of the individual." They have to start by looking at freedom as a right of all of nature. Thus they must free everything which makes life possible: the air, the waters, the trees, everything the holy web of life depends on.

APPEAL OF THE HAUDENOSAUNEE TO THE WESTERN WORLD.

MANDALA:

Whirlpool where the four corners stream from. Apache Native Americans.

How happy am I? That is the most important question for us in life. For an Native American success does not depend on how much money he or she earns, nor on his (or her) social status - but solely on how happy he (or she) is.

BERYL BLUE SPRUCE, PUEBLO NATIVE AMERICAN WOMAN

MANDALA:

Collage from mystical symbols of the Ojibwa Native Americans.

If you see one
one my children
then value every single
one
of them
for what he is:
a child of our father
in heaven
and your brother.

CHIEF DAN GEORGE

MANDALA:

Weaving of the Yokut
Native Americans

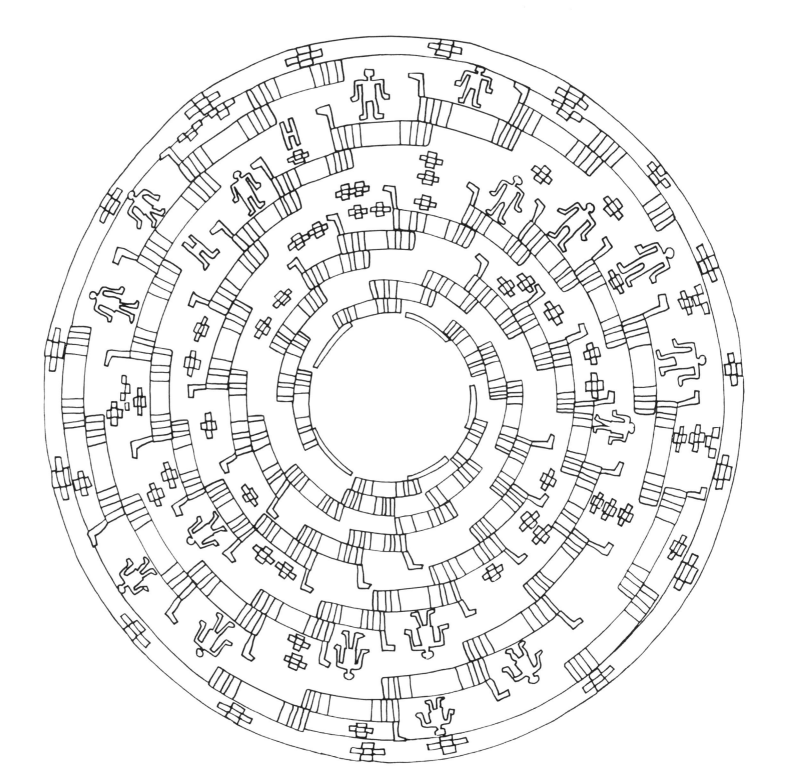

He who cannot love
himself
cannot love anybody.
He who is ashamed of his
body
is ashamed in all matters
of life.
He who regards his body
as dirty
is lost.
He who cannot respect
the gifts
given to him before birth
can never have
true respect for anything.

A NOOTKA NATIVE AMERICAN
WOMAN

MANDALA:

Image of a falcon
Pueblo Native Americans

When God created the
land
of the Native Americans,
it was
as if he spread a large
blanket
whereupon he placed the
Native Americans.
I did not come here
from a foreign country,
I was put here
by the creator.

CHIEF WENINOCK, YAKIMA

MANDALA:

Weaving of the Cahnilla
Native Americans

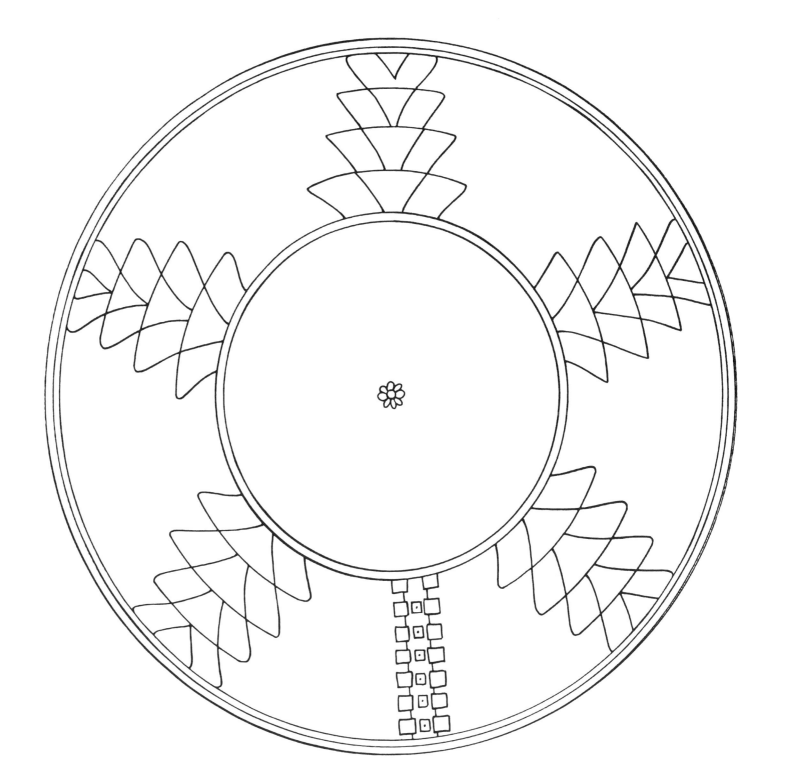

If you want to be a medi-
cine man you must have
experienced everything.
If did not experience the
human side of everything,
how then can you teach
or heal?
In order to be a good
medicine man you must
be humble.
You must be deeper than
a worm and higher than
an eagle.

Archie Fire Lame Deer,
Lakota

MANDALA:

Head-dress of the Haida
Native Americans, seen
from above.

You are asking me,
but I know nothing about
death;
I only got to know life.
I can only say
what I do believe:
either death is the end of
life
or the transition to
a different form of life.
In no case is there any-
thing
to be afraid of.

An Innuit woman (Eskimo)

Mandala:

Rising rain deity, Hopi

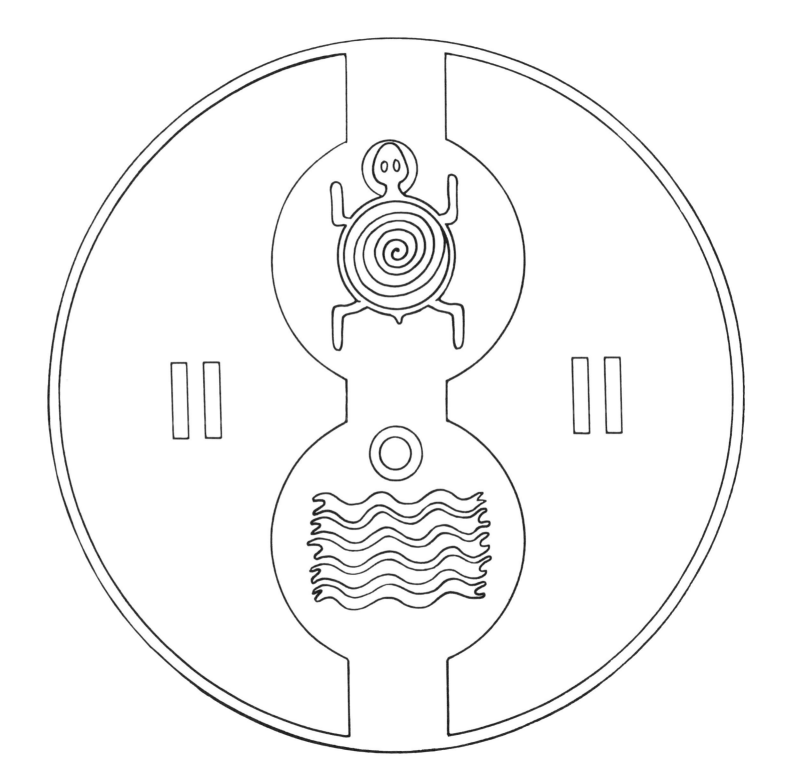

Whenever the red
hunter discovers
something in his wander-
ings
that is impressive and
sublime (noble)
he stops for a moment
in devout silence.
To him it is not necessary
to honor one of seven
days
everyday is holy
to him.

OHIYESA, SIOUX

MANDALA:

Shield of the Plains
Native Americans

My grandfather faced
me
downwards to the earth
so it would give me its
gifts;
Then he held me facing
up
to the sky
so a life in harmony
would be granted to me.

ALONZO LOPEZ, PAPAGO

MANDALA:

Labyrinth of the Papago
Native Americans

The birds leave the earth
with the help of their
wings.
Human beings too can
leave the earth, though
not with their wings
but with their spirit.

HEHAKA SAPA, SIOUX

MANDALA:

Weaving of the Hopi, rep-
resenting a bird.

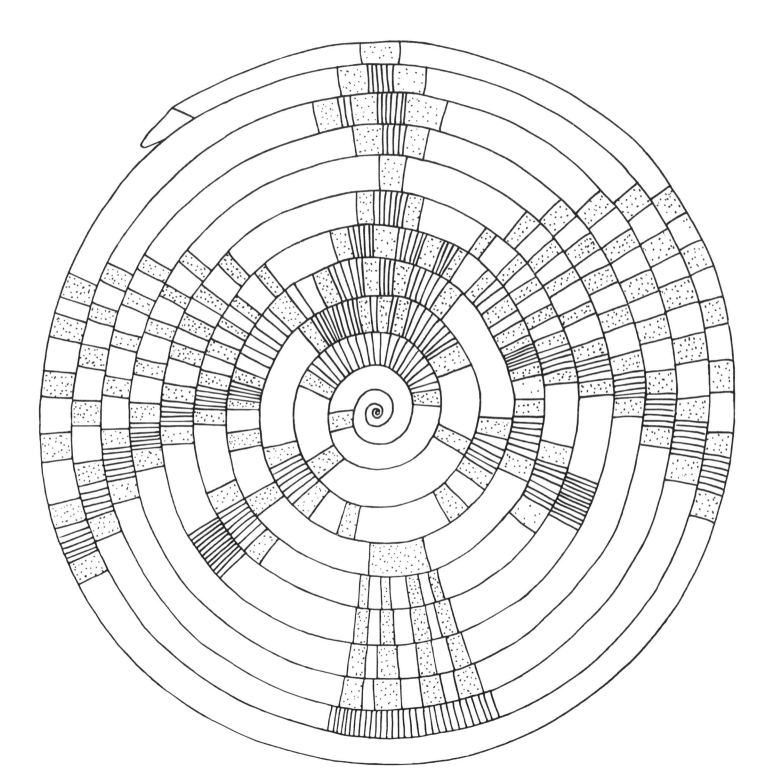

There lays a world
beyond our own,
a world which is far away
very close and invisible.
And it is there where
God lives and the dead
reside
the ghosts and the saints
a world where everything
has already happened and
everything
is known.
This world speaks.
It has its own language.

MARIA SABINA, FEMALE SHAMAN
OF THE MAZAKETA

MANDALA:

Sun Symbol of the
Huichiol Native
Americans